1689: The Siege of Londonderry. The city gates are shut against James II's (Catholic) army

1690: The Battle of the Boyne. William III arrives and defeats James II

1704: Penal Laws. William III imposes harsh restrictions on Catholics

1654: 'To hell or to Connaught'. Irish landowners are forced to move west

1646: Battle of Benburb. Owen Roe O'Neill wins victory over the Scottish

1641: The Great Rebellion, Ulster

1649: Oliver Cromwell lays claim over Ireland by winning battles at Drogheda and Wexford

1605: Flight of the Earls. Earls facing exile flee as English and Scots settle

1541: Henry VIII declares himself King of Ireland and sends settlers to establish Protestantism

1459: The Pale declares itself free of English laws

1569-1583: Constant rebellions against Elizabeth I's control

1592: Ireland's first University, Trinity College, Dublin, is set up

1594-1603: Hugh O'Neill's 9-year war to prevent the English from taking his land

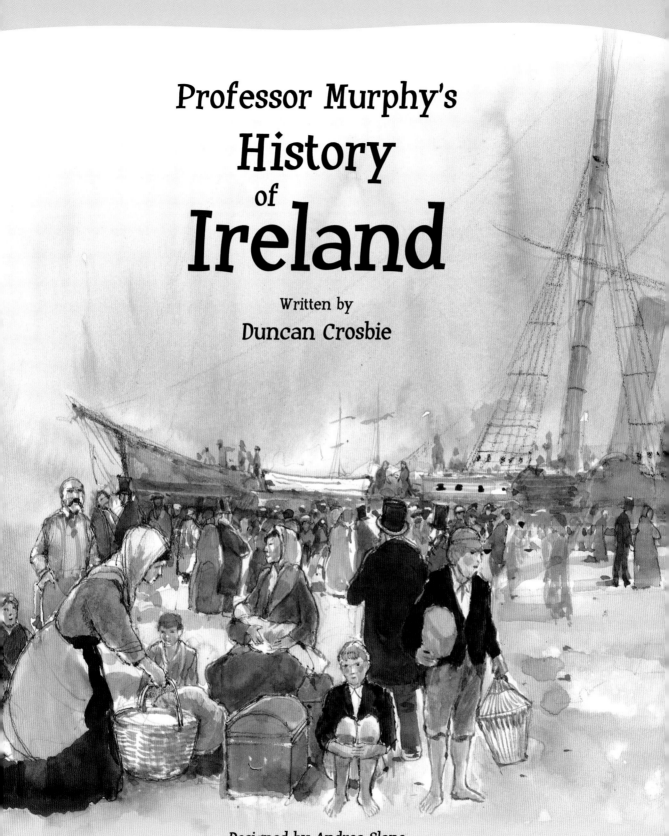

Professor Murphy's
History
of
Ireland

Written by
Duncan Crosbie

Designed by Andrea Slane

Illustrated by Anthony Morris and Karen Donnelly

Edited by Dee Costello and Lisa Regan

Contents

Chapter 11
Nationalism on the march (1850–1914) Part 2

Chapter 12
War of Independence & Irish Free State (1916–1923)

Chapter 13
Partition & Republic (1923–1960s)

Chapter 14
Economic & social liberation (1960s–present)

Chapter 15
The Troubles & their resolution (1960s–present)

Hello!
I'm Professor Murphy.

Do you like to hear true stories about men and women from the past, about battles and revolutions, great ideas and brave movements?

I hope you do because that's what I've written about in this book. You will find out about Ireland's history, from ancient times to the present day. I'll come with you on your journey, too, and talk you through the main themes of each chapter.

I've also included an illustrated timeline from my notes (at the front and back of this book) to help you understand the order of important events.

Now, read on and enjoy!

The first settlers

Professor Murphy here! I'm going to tell you all about us, the Irish – who we are, where we come from and the things that have happened to us.

As far as we know, the first Stone Age settlers arrived about the time the Ice Age was ending and rising sea levels cut Ireland off from Britain, surrounding it with water. These people were always on the move, gathering berries, catching fish and birds and hunting animals like wolves and boar with stone-tipped spears. They cut skin and meat with the sharp edges of flakes of stone, set into a wooden handle.

Around 4,000 BC people of what we call the New Stone Age arrived, probably in boats made of wood and animal skins, bringing cattle, pigs, goats – and better tools. With sharp stone axes they cleared the trees, began to farm and built fortified villages.

As well as hilltop villages, island dwellings were built. These are known as crannógs and are huts made on small sections of land, surrounded by water.

Famous settlements

🌀 The earliest settlement (about 7,000–6,500 BC) discovered in Ireland is at Mount Sandel, near Coleraine, Co. Derry.

🌀 Near Ballycastle in Co. Mayo are the Céide Fields, a New Stone Age field system dating back to about 3,000 BC.

🌀 More than 200,000 tonnes of stone was used to build Newgrange passage grave and it was all done without machines!

Hunting for meat

Excavations around the huts near Mount Sandel have uncovered cooked bones of wild pig, freshwater fish such as salmon and trout, as well as hare and bird. What a hungry bunch!

Amazing passage graves

The New Stone Age people left extraordinary monuments: great stone tombs for the dead, covered by mounds of earth. You can still see many remains of the four kinds: court cairns, passage graves, dolmens and wedge tombs. The most spectacular passage graves are in Co. Meath – at Newgrange, Dowth, Knowth and on the Hill of Tara.

Newgrange is 85m across and 15m high. Inside is a 19m passage of massive upright stones leading to three chambers, all roofed with more heavy slabs and still watertight thousands of years later. There are decorative carvings made without any iron tools, and the engineering is so exact that on the shortest day each year, 21st December, the sun reaches through the little doorway to light up the central chamber.

Detail of stone carvings at Newgrange entrance

Newgrange was built in about 3,200 BC, so it had its 5,000th birthday quite a while ago. It is older than Stonehenge in England and the pyramids of ancient Egypt!

Different tribes often raided each other to steal slaves and cattle.

find out more at www.mythicalireland.com/ancientsites

Coming of the Gaels and their language

Nobody knows when the first Celts, or Gaels, arrived in Ireland, but it was probably around 500 BC. They kept on coming in the next few hundred years and conquered all the original inhabitants. They were great warriors, but also believers in fair and just laws for everybody, including the tribal kings. The law treated women well and they shared wealth and property with their husbands.

The main social groups were aristocrats, freemen and slaves (usually captured in battle). The most important people were warriors (flaithi in Gaelic), lawyers (brehons), historians (seanchaithe), poets (filí) and druids (draci).

To begin with there were about 150 small kingdoms, but by AD 400 there were five main areas – Ulster (Ulaid), Leinster (Laigin), Munster (Muma), Connaught (Connacht), and Meath and Westmeath (Midhe).

Connacht

Midhe

Laigin

Muma

There were no schools. Instead, the Gaels often fostered their children with other families to learn everything they needed to know about daily life.

Age of great Irish legends

Later, Christian monks wrote down both the Brehon laws of the Gaels and their exciting stories. These sagas tell us about the things the Gaels believed in or did. Cuchulain, for example, is a heroic warrior who always fights fairly and behaves honourably. The Cattle Raid of Cooley (Táin Bó Cuailgne) tells of the battles between Cuchulain of Ulster and Queen Méabh of Connaught. This body of tales comes from the Ulster Cycle, one of four major cycles of Irish mythology. The other three are Kings, Fionn and Mythological.

As time passed, most of these legends were forgotten. But as men and women of the 19th century began to look forward to an independent Ireland, sagas like those of Cuchulain, or of Fionn Mac Cumhaill and his Fenian warriors, became important and inspiring.

Irish mythology

Ⓖ Cycle of the Kings is a collection of early Irish tales. It tells of the reign of kings from the 6th–8th centuries.

Ⓖ Ulster Cycle (Rúraíocht) tells heroic tales associated with Ulster. In addition to Táin Bó Cuailgne, there are many other stories such as Deirdre and the sons of Uisneach.

Ⓖ Fionn Cycle (Fiannaíocht) tells a series of hunting tales primarily to do with warrior Fionn Mac Cumhaill. The love story of Diarmuid and Gráinne, also in this collection, may be the origin of the European tale of Tristan and Isolde.

Ⓖ Mythological Cycle narrates early Irish adventures of the gods and goddesses of Ireland.

The Gaels had no money. How well off you were depended on how many cattle you had.

Legends of the land

Ⓖ According to legend, the great poet Cir went to the northern kingdom, and the great harpist Cennfin to the southern. Maybe that's why poetry is strong in the north and music in the south.

Ⓖ The Hill of Tara, Co. Meath, was the ancient seat of power. The standing stone, or 'stone of destiny', is said to have cried out when the rightful king of Ireland touched it.

find out more at www.ict.mic.ul.ie/2003/phealy/site/History.htm

Arrival of Christianity

Round about AD 400 traders were going backwards and forwards to Britain and the continent buying and selling. They brought back news of events and important ideas, such as Christianity.

Christian ideas spread slowly through Europe in the four centuries after the death of Jesus. There must have been missionaries already working in Ireland because, in 431, the Pope sent Palladius as the first bishop. St Patrick is the most famous missionary. Unlike the others, he wrote about his life and work – although, he didn't tell us much about the widespread paganism in Ireland or what year he arrived! It may have been about 456.

St Patrick didn't try to force people to accept Christianity. Instead, he made friends and told Christian stories. It took about 200 years for the whole country to be converted to Christianity.

Legend has it that St Patrick used the shamrock's three leaves to explain the Trinity. Much later it became a national symbol.

About St Patrick

🔄 St Patrick was born in Britain, possibly near Bristol, and was captured by Irish slave traders when he was 16. He escaped after six years, became a priest and returned to Ireland.

🔄 He is supposed to have driven the snakes out of Ireland, never to return. This legend is said to illustrate that pagan beliefs, or 'snakes', had been destroyed.

🔄 Pagan beliefs were held by Pre-Christian Europe and are not part of any of the world's major religions.

Irish scholars and monasteries

Between 500 and 800, a great many monasteries were founded. In them, monks and scholars established a golden age of learning and artistic achievement. The rest of Europe was suffering constant warfare between tribes and kingdoms, many of them pagan. This period was called the Dark Ages. But hundreds of outstanding Irish scholars and missionaries set out to keep Christianity alive in France, Spain, Germany and Italy.

For example St Colm Cille, or Columba to the Scots, brought Christianity to Scotland by founding the monastic school of Iona. From there it spread southwards into England. Soon after, St Columbanus (543–615) travelled through France, Switzerland and Italy setting up monasteries in which the library was important because it kept books and learning safe.

St Colm Cille (521–597) is the patron saint of poets.

Irish monasteries

Ⓖ Irish monasteries created world famous treasures like the *Book of Durrow* (6th century), the Ardagh chalice and the beautiful *Book of Kells* (both 8th century).

Ⓖ Among the first is St Enda's monastery on Árainn, Innishmore, Aran Islands.

Ⓖ St Finnian's at Clonard, Co. Meath is believed to be the starting point for many other monastery founders.

To begin with, monasteries were collections of small wooden huts grouped around a church. Stone buildings came later, and there was a good reason. Viking raids!

find out more at www.monasticireland.com/storiesofsaints/colmcille.htm

The coming of the Vikings

A nasty shock was waiting for people all over western Europe – the Vikings! The first raid was on the English monastery of Lindisfarne in 793, but it only took two years for the Vikings to work their way round the coast and make a start on Ireland.

To begin with, the Vikings were hunting two things – treasure and slaves. The churches and monasteries were irresistible because that was where they found silver crosses and other religious ornaments – and monks, to kidnap and sell as slaves in Britain, France, Spain and north Africa.

By the 840s the Vikings had established winter bases around the coast in places that would later grow into major towns – Wexford, Waterford, Limerick, Cork and Dubh Linn, or Dublin. Some of the small Irish kingdoms joined forces to drive the Vikings back but, in 914, a huge fleet arrived in Waterford. This time the Vikings intended to stay as settlers. The wooden churches and monasteries had been destroyed so many times that now they were being rebuilt in stone.

There were lots of great treasures.

Why stone towers?

🜨 The monasteries built tall stone alarm towers in which to store their treasures safe from attack. The door was 3m above the ground, and not even Vikings were that tall!

🜨 These round stone towers are unique to Ireland. Many still exist at places like Glendalough, Cashel and Monasterboice.

Vikings travelled overseas in their longships and gained a reputation as fierce warriors.

Vikings were invaders from Scandinavia. They were keen raiders, traders and settlers in the coastal areas of northern Europe and beyond from c.9th–11th centuries.

Great shipbuilders

⑨ The Dublin Vikings were master shipbuilders. The remains of a sea dragon, or warship, built there in 1042 were found a few years ago in Denmark.

⑨ The ship was rebuilt using 300 oak trees. It was named the *Sea Stallion* and sailed from Denmark to Dublin in 2007. It returned to Denmark in 2008 to go in the Viking Ship Museum at Roskilde.

Traders and settlers

During the 10th century the Vikings settled down and established Dublin as an important trading city. They were expert shipbuilders and sailed far and wide trading leather, jewels, metal goods and, as usual, slaves. They traded with the native Irish as well, and there were many fights with the local chieftains. For example, Dublin was successfully invaded thirteen times during the 10th century. Even so, King Anlaf Sihtricsson (or Amlaíb Cuarán) ruled there for over 30 years and was the first to make his own coins, a sign of stability.

Viking Dublin was crowded, busy, smelly and lively, with timber houses built of wattles, each with a little patch of ground around it, and roads made of split tree trunks.

Viking Dublin was a hive of activity.

find out more at www.lore-and-saga.co.uk/html/viking_ships.html

The Vikings join in

The history of Ireland is all a bit of a muddle in the 11th and 12th centuries. Everyone seems to be wandering around fighting. Sometimes you get the feeling that tribal chiefs must have formed a queue at Tara to wait their turn to be high king...

Once the Vikings had settled down to live as traders in Ireland, they began to intermarry and adopt Christianity. They also joined in the fighting that went on most of the time as different families and kingdoms tried to become top dog.

Although there were up to a hundred small kingdoms, called tuaths, who elected their own kings, there were also a few larger kingdoms, called tuaithe, controlled by powerful families like the O'Neills in the north and the O'Connors in the west. Vikings from one town might join forces with this or that small kingdom, while Vikings from another town took different sides. So the Dublin Vikings, for example, sometimes joined forces with the men of Leinster to rebel against the power of the O'Neills.

Many Vikings married the native Irish.

Interesting facts

🔗 The O'Neills of Ulster were the chief family in the north for many centuries – from the early years of Gaelic settlement until the 'Flight of the Earls' in 1607. (See chapter 6.)

🔗 The chief of a tribe was called toisech. From that word comes the modern name for a prime minister – taoiseach.

Brian Bórú and his battles

Brian Bórú, from Boroimhe in Co. Clare, spent the first half of his life pushing the Vikings out of Munster and back into their southern towns.

In 968 he helped his brother Mahon to recapture the Rock of Cashel, the seat of Munster kings. By 976 he was King of Munster himself, but had to fight many battles to keep and increase his power. His rival as possible High King of Ireland was Mael Sechnaill of Tara. Mael knew he had little chance against a famous warrior like Brian and submitted to him in 1002. But unless the O'Neills of Ulster obeyed him the title 'High King' meant nothing. For the next 12 years Brian was constantly fighting and making alliances until, at last, he commanded obedience from (almost) everybody.

**Brian Bórú
(941–1014)**

The Rock of Cashel, Co. Tipperary, is an exceptional limestone outcrop that could be defended easily.

Brian Bórú

Ⓖ Brian Bórú was the twelfth son of his father, Cennétig. As a child he saw his mother, Bé Binn, murdered by Viking raiders.

Ⓖ In 1005, Brian Bórú declared that Armagh was the religious capital of all Ireland. In return, the Book of Armagh named him 'Emperor of the Irish'.

find out more at www.dochara.com/the-irish/ireland-history/vikings

Battle of Clontarf

The men of Leinster never enjoyed being under somebody else's thumb, whether the thumb belonged to Ulster or Munster. In 1014 they joined forces (again) with the Dublin Vikings, brought in a thousand extra warriors from Norway and the Isle of Man and met Brian Bórú's army at Clontarf, now a suburb of Dublin. It was the greatest battle on Irish soil and the Vikings were driven into the sea and drowned.

Brian was victorious, but was killed in his tent after the battle. He is one of the great figures of Irish history who (like the legendary Cuchulain) was remembered as a noble and courageous warrior hero – but he was also the man who rebuilt the monasteries in Munster and re-established learning after the destruction of war.

According to legend, as Brodir, King of Man, fled from the battle he killed Brian Bórú. Brodir was caught and tortured to death.

About 7,000 fought with Brian Bórú and more than half were killed. Of the Leinster-Viking army of 8,000, it is said only 2,000 were left alive.

From Clontarf to the Normans

It's easy to think of Brian Bórú as the man who made Ireland a nation, but people didn't think like that then. Their ambition was to gain power and wealth for one region or one family over the others. Brian Bórú was simply the best warrior and wisest man of his time. After Clontarf the Vikings were never again a problem, but soon the different kingdoms were fighting each other once more.

For 150 years things were almost as muddled as they had been before Brian until, in 1152, Dermot MacMurrough (or Diarmuid MacMurchú), King of Leinster, ran off with the wife of another king, Tigernán Ó Ruairc. Ó Ruairc swore revenge and, although he had to wait, in 1166 he forced Dermot to flee abroad...and Irish history changed for ever.

Dermot MacMurrough (1110–1171) ran off with the wife of the king of Bréifne.

High crosses

ⓖ High crosses are large stone sculptures. They are recognised as one of Ireland's greatest contributions to the art of medieval Europe.

ⓖ Monastic art reached its peak when, in 1123, the magnificent gold, silver and copper Cross of Cong was created for the King of Connaught.

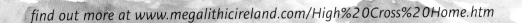

find out more at www.megalithicireland.com/High%20Cross%20Home.htm

Strongbow's arrival

The King of England, Henry II, was busy fighting in France when Dermot MacMurrough asked for help to recover his lands. After thinking about it, Henry thought this might be a chance to add to his own kingdom. He sent knights led by 'Strongbow', whose real name was Richard de Clare.

Henry II
(1154–1189)

Strongbow wasn't going to solve Dermot's problems without a large reward. Strongbow married Dermot's daughter, Aoife, and made him promise that, when he died, Strongbow would be the next king of Leinster.

Between May and September 1170, a small Norman army won a battle at Baginbun, Co. Wexford, and captured Waterford and Dublin. Armoured cavalry and archers who could fire 12 arrows a minute were unknown to the Irish, and they had no effective way of protecting themselves.

Why did Dermot MacMurrough running away from Ireland change our history for ever? You could explain it in one word – Normans! In 1066 they invaded England and their leader, William the Conqueror, made himself king. But they were hungry for more land, and when Dermot asked for their help they couldn't wait to climb into their ships and head for Ireland.

The Normans were originally Vikings who had settled in northern France 250 years earlier.

Fascinating facts

Strongbow is believed to have died from an injury to his foot in April 1176.

ⓖ The Pope wanted to reform the Church in Ireland and organise it on the same lines as the rest of Europe. This was difficult without a powerful king at the centre, and was why the Pope backed Henry II of England.

ⓖ The mighty longbow, that could fire arrows up to 200m, was not yet in use, but smaller bows were devastating against soldiers without plate armour.

Henry II gets worried

Strongbow's small army was so successful that Henry II began to worry. He didn't want Strongbow to become powerful enough to rule Ireland himself so, in 1171, he ordered him back to England. At that very moment, Dermot died and Strongbow became king of Leinster. Henry II immediately brought a large army to Ireland. He made Strongbow submit to him and then, very cleverly, called a meeting of bishops at the Rock of Cashel. They all accepted Henry, and the Pope was so pleased he gave him the title 'Lord of Ireland'.

His warm welcome and his strong army made it difficult for other Irish kings to resist Henry. In 1175 Rory O'Connor of Connaught, who had claimed Leinster for himself, swore loyalty to King Henry as his overlord.

Christ Church Cathedral

One of the first buildings begun by the Normans was Christ Church Cathedral in Dublin.

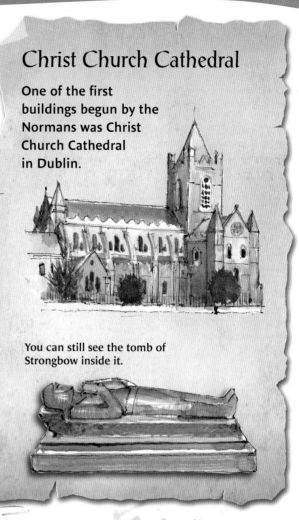

You can still see the tomb of Strongbow inside it.

find out more at www.irelandinformationguide.com/Diarmuid_MacMorrough

The Normans are here to stay

Norman knights came to Ireland to seize land and become rich, and with their superior military weapons and tactics they quickly succeeded. By 1250, three quarters of Ireland was controlled by them. Everything about the Normans was different. They brought new laws that allowed one person to own lands, unlike the traditional Brehon law that said land belonged to the whole family or tribe.

They made sure Norman law was followed by building castles, both large and small, in many parts of the country. They fortified towns, and built new ones surrounded by stone walls – in places like Athenry, Drogheda, Galway and New Ross. The only parts of Ireland not under Norman control by 1250 were west Ulster and parts of Connaught.

King John's Castle in Limerick was a Norman fortress of the early 13th century. It was kept ready for the king's army to move into if there was trouble.

Brehon law was a legal system of early medieval Ireland. It was created by jurists rather than kings.

The first Norman castles were built quickly with wooden walls on top of earth banks. Later they were rebuilt in stone, like Dundrum Castle, Co. Down (1180 onwards).

Norman integration

The first Irish parliament met in 1264 but it represented only the Normans living in towns, and not Norman lords or native Irish people in the countryside.

Brian O'Neill of Ulster tried to organise an anti-Norman rebellion in 1258; a Norman army was defeated and FitzThomas, Lord Desmond, was killed at the Battle of Callan in 1261; and in 1315 Edward Bruce brought an army from Scotland. The O'Connor kings of Connaught also rebelled but in 1316 they, and five other Irish kings, were killed at the Battle of Athenry. Within a year Edward controlled Ireland north of Dublin, but his soldiers behaved so badly that he lost support and was killed in 1318 at the Battle of Faughart. The O'Neills re-emerged as a dominant force.

Normans slowly began to marry Irish people, learn the Irish language and wear Irish clothes. It was said they started to become 'more Irish than the Irish themselves'.

Edward Bruce

Ⓖ Edward Bruce's fleet landed in Co. Antrim in 1315 and his expedition lasted three years. He called himself 'King of Ireland'.

Ⓖ Edward became so hated that after he was killed the Annals of Ulster said: 'there was not done from the beginning of the world a deed that was better for the Men of Ireland'.

Edward Bruce
(1280–1318)

find out more at www.teachnet.ie/mmorrin/castle/index.htm

The Black Death

By the time the Normans had been in Ireland for about 200 years, they had lost some of the lands they had conquered. In fact many of them had learned Irish, adopted local customs and were now called the 'Old English'. What was left of the English royal power base was part of Leinster around Dublin. It was known as The Pale and, in theory, native Irish were not supposed to go into it.

Bubonic plague (known as the Black Death from the colour of the lumps that grew on its victims) spread from the east all the way across Europe, killing millions slowly and painfully. It reached Ireland in 1348, carried by rats and fleas arriving on merchant ships. The fleas sucked the blood of infected rats and then preyed on humans, passing on the disease.

The Black Death killed one third of the population of England and although nobody counted the Irish dead, it was probably about the same. 'There was hardly a house in which only one died,' wrote a Kilkenny monk. This puts the disaster on a similar scale to the Great Famine 500 years later. For the next 50 years outbreaks of the plague continued to strike.

After the Black Death, trade came to an almost complete stop, so English kings lost interest in Ireland. In any case they had troubles of their own...

Entire villages were deserted and lands went to waste.

How did it spread?

ⓢ The Black Death spread along trade routes. It hit Dublin in August 1348 and quickly moved into rural areas. It reached Moylurg, Co. Roscommon by 1349.

ⓢ The population of Europe in 1400 was half what it had been at the start of 1345, the year the Black Death first struck the continent.

The dead often lay unburied for days because people were scared of being infected. Sometimes the priests died and proper burial services could not be held.

Statutes of Kilkenny

In 1337 the Hundred Years War with France began, and there were no spare soldiers to send to Ireland to help the Norman rulers inside the Dublin Pale. Increasingly, these men were worried by the way the 'Old English' were becoming Irish so, in 1366, they issued the Statutes of Kilkenny. These banned Brehon laws, the Irish language, Irish dress, manners, hair styles and even the Irish style of riding a horse! Nobody outside the Pale took much notice. The most powerful men in the land, like the Earl of Desmond, were now thoroughly Irish and nobody could tell them how to behave.

An Irish revival

Ⓖ As the Gaelic revival got underway, old traditions were brought back and important literary works, such as *Leabhar Breac* (*The Speckled Book*), were written (1408–11).

Ⓖ The Irish seanchaithe – historians – came into their own as in the old days, recording events with great attention to their truthfulness and accuracy.

find out more at www.eyewitnesstohistory.com/plague.htm

Revival of Gaelic power

During a quiet period in the Hundred Years War, Richard II made two expeditions to Ireland in the 1390s to try to restore the power of the English crown. He failed. By now some of the native Irish chieftains, as well as Old English noblemen, controlled large areas of land and ruled over them without challenge.

During the next hundred years three major families began to control most of Ireland – the Earls of Desmond in the south-west, the Earls of Ormonde in the centre and, most powerful of all, the Earls of Kildare in the east. By 1470 the 7th Earl of Kildare had become chief governor of Ireland. In theory, he acted on behalf of the King of England. In fact, he ruled like a king himself.

Richard II
(1367–1400)

Leading families

Leading families like the Desmonds, Ormondes, Kildares, O'Neills and O'Donnells built stone towers and forts wherever they might need them for protection. You can still find the ruins of over 2,000 in Ireland.

Stone tower

Map showing areas where the Earls ruled

Earls of Kildare

Earls of Ormonde

Earls of Desmond

'Silken Thomas' and five of his uncles were beheaded at the Tower of London, in 1537.

The first plantations

Henry VIII declared that 'his' lands in Ireland had been stolen, that he was not getting any rent from them and that he intended to take them back. At almost the same moment, England broke away from Rome and the Catholic Church.

In 1534, 'Silken Thomas' 10th Earl of Kildare and five of his uncles rebelled, but they were defeated and the power of the mighty Kildares was finished for good. Henry had himself declared King of Ireland in 1541 and introduced the policy of Surrender and Regrant: surrender my rightful lands and I, Henry, will grant them back to you — if you swear loyalty (and pay the rent).

To make sure Ireland outside the Pale was thoroughly anglicised, Henry and his successors sent English settlers to establish 'plantations' of Protestants.

If it wasn't the Hundred Years War keeping royal English noses out of Ireland, it was their own civil war, the Wars of the Roses. But it was all too good to last, and when the Tudors grabbed the English crown in 1485 it was bad news for Ireland. Henry VII loved making money and Henry VIII loved spending it — which meant he was always after more. And that spelt trouble...

Henry VIII
(1491–1547)

The Tudor period relates to the royal family of England ruling between 1485–1603.

The Tudor plantations was a policy adopted for 'reforming' Ireland of the 'wild' Irish.

Who's in charge?

🅖 In 1459, the Irish parliament in the Pale declared itself free of any laws made in England unless it agreed to them. Nobody outside the Pale paid much attention.

🅖 Before Henry VIII got involved, there were more than 60 kings, princes and chiefs controlling their own separate regions within Ireland.

🅖 The Irish Reformation Parliament of 1536 banned saffron-yellow clothes, long hair, moustaches, Irish poets and harpists — and, as usual, the language.

find out more at www.historylearningsite.co.uk/henry_viii_ireland.htm

Rebellion and plantation

> The old Gaelic kings and chieftains, and the Old English aristocrats, now held their lands according to the English king's law, not the Brehon law. For a while they assumed the Tudor kings were just one of those annoying things you have to put up with. Elizabeth I had different ideas...

Queen Elizabeth I
(1533–1603)

Elizabeth was determined to enforce absolute control over the whole of Ireland. Once the various Irish rulers realised she intended to control all their lands, and hoped to convert the Irish church to Protestantism, most of them (but not all) rebelled.

Her reign saw continuous battles and fighting. Shane O'Neill led the revolt in Ulster until he was murdered in 1567. In Munster the Catholic Desmonds led almost constant rebellions against Elizabeth and Protestantism from 1569–1583, with only a short period of peace in the middle. When Elizabeth's army finally beat the Desmonds, their lands were seized and given to plantations of English Protestant settlers. The brutality of this period sowed lasting hatreds, but it also ensured the Irish church held fast to Catholicism.

Frightful facts

☻ Baron Grey de Wilton ordered the massacre of over 600 Spanish and Italian Catholics during the siege of Smerwick in 1580. People in Europe were as horrified by this as by the St Bartholomew's Day Massacre of Protestants in Paris, France, in 1572.

☻ Queen Elizabeth confiscated rebels' lands in the plantations of Munster. They were cleared of Irish inhabitants and replaced with English settlers.

Ireland's first university, Trinity College, Dublin, was set up in 1592. For the first 30 years of its life it accepted both Catholics and Protestants.

Hugh O'Neill

Hugh O'Neill was the last great Gaelic chieftain to make a stand against English attempts to take his lands. He had spent many years at Elizabeth I's court, he had fought in her armies and she made him Earl of Tyrone in 1585. But he became convinced that she wanted to control his Ulster like the rest of Ireland and, in 1598, he won the battles of Clontibret and Yellow Ford.

The Catholic King of Spain promised military help and, in 1600, O'Neill marched south to join forces with Spanish troops at Kinsale in Co. Cork. By now 20,000 English troops were in Ireland, and O'Neill was quickly defeated. He finally surrendered in 1603, fled to Italy in 1607 and died in Rome in 1616.

Rebellion and war

☺ Rebel leader Hugh O'Neill (1550–1616) was engaged in a nine-year war, 1594–1603.

☺ During the Desmond rebellions, Hugh O'Neill had fought on the side of the English against the Munster chieftains.

☺ In 1607 O'Neill sailed into exile from Rathmullan, Co. Donegal, with Rory O'Donnell, Earl of Tyrconnell, and almost 100 other Gaelic chieftains. This was later called 'The Flight of the Earls'.

When the Spaniards landed in Kinsale they were besieged by the English army.

O'Neill's army had marched in the depths of winter from Ulster to Kinsale.

find out more at www.flightoftheearls.ie/background.htm

The plantation of Ulster

The Flight of the Earls was the end of Gaelic Ireland. From now on it was to be English law that governed everything. After 40 years of rebellion, fighting and slaughter the English weren't very popular, and things were about to get a whole lot worse!

Scots had been crossing the sea and settling in eastern Ulster for many years, but once O'Neill had gone there was a rush of English and Scottish to settle on his lands. Within 15 years, nearly 20,000 Protestant settlers were 'planted' on land confiscated from Catholics. New towns were built, and the original Irish were forced into small pockets of land, paying high rents for what had once been theirs.

Earlier invaders like the Vikings and Normans had settled down and eventually become Irish themselves. Now, religion was the great barrier. All over Europe, Catholics and Protestants looked on each other with hatred and fear. In Ulster, the new settlers regarded the Irish as enemies to be harshly controlled, and centuries of mistrust began between the Protestant and Catholic inhabitants.

Natives of the affected areas found their stake in the settlement reduced greatly, which caused discontent. The English and Scots were given lands on favourable terms.

Local population

Ⓢ The City of London financed the development of the new county of Derry. It rebuilt the old town of Derry and renamed it Londonderry.

Ⓢ In Co. Derry the Irish were resettled in about 10% of the land and paid rents that were twice as high as those paid by the settlers.

Ⓢ Migration resulted in a settler population of some 40,000 in Ulster by 1640.

The Great Rebellion of 1641

The English kings were determined to seize the lands of the leading Old English and Gaelic Irish families (who were mainly Catholics). The English parliament was determined that only Protestants could have power and wealth – what was later called the 'Protestant Ascendancy'. So the Old English and Gaelic Irish were bitterly opposed to the New English, and this led to the bloodiest century in Irish history.

At Clongowes Castle, Co. Kildare, Protestants killed women, children and soldiers even after they had surrendered.

Things came to a head in the 1640s and 1650s. A great rebellion was planned for 1641, and although some of the Dublin leaders were betrayed and arrested it went ahead in Ulster, where the bitterness was greatest. There was terrible bloodshed in which about 12,000 Protestants died. Following the success of the rebellion, exiled Catholics returned to Ireland to continue the fight.

Portadown bridge

One of the worst incidents of the Ulster rebellion was the massacre on Portadown bridge, in which about 100 men, women and children were brutally killed. The memory is still alive today.

find out more at www.plantationofulster.org

Confederation of Kilkenny

You would hardly believe it, but no sooner had the Great Rebellion started in Ireland than the English parliament turned on the king, Charles I. In no time the two sides were knocking lumps out of each other in a long civil war, and had little time to find sensible solutions to the problems in Ireland. Mind you, Oliver Cromwell was learning to become a soldier...

Once again, the O'Neills emerged as leaders. Sir Phelim had led the Ulster rebellion and, in 1642, Owen Roe O'Neill returned from Spain to take charge of Irish forces. In the same year the Old English lords, the returned Irish exiles and the Catholic churchmen met at Kilkenny. 'Confederation' means to form an alliance and the Supreme Council often met in Kilkenny, hence the name 'Confederation of Kilkenny'. Surprisingly, they agreed on loyalty to Charles I, but unsurprisingly they opposed the puritan Protestants – two things Oliver Cromwell would not forget in years to come.

Owen Roe O'Neill
(1590–1649)

What the returning exiles and the Old English most wanted was their old lands. This allowed Owen Roe O'Neill, an experienced soldier, to control most of Ireland, and in 1646 he won a great victory against a Scottish army at the Battle of Benburb in Co. Tyrone. This was seen as a victory for Charles I.

King Charles I
(1600–1649)

Very bloody facts

☺ In England, King Charles I lost the civil war against the parliamentary side, and in January 1649 he was publicly executed. Strict, rigorous Puritans now ruled the country.

☺ Although 12,000 Ulster Protestants were brutally murdered in 1641, exaggerated stories reached England. One said 150,000 had been killed – more than the Protestant population of the whole of Ireland – and this led to demands for revenge.

'Like a lightning through the land'

The 8,000 English and Scottish soldiers stranded in Ireland after Benburb took refuge in fortified towns like Drogheda. In August 1649, Cromwell arrived with another 12,000 soldiers and a good supply of cannon and other weapons.

During the next two months, he made his name the most hated in Irish history. In September he besieged Drogheda, and slaughtered nearly 3,500 soldiers, women and children, calling it 'a righteous judgement of God'. In October, his army did much the same at Wexford. At least 2,000 were killed in Wexford and those not killed in Drogheda and Wexford were sent to Barbados as slaves. In his own mind, he was avenging the massacres of Protestants in 1641, but he was also trying to make sure that no-one would dare oppose English rule in future. Owen Roe O'Neill was the only man who might have done so, but he died suddenly in November 1649.

Drogheda had taken no part in the Great Rebellion of 1641, but it was a royalist town and had supported Charles I. Many of the soldiers murdered after they surrendered were English and Scottish.

Some 2,000–3,000 defenders were killed in the attack on Drogheda, plus some civilians.

find out more at www.doyle.com.au/cromwell.htm

'The curse of Cromwell'

Oliver Cromwell
(1599–1658)

Having subdued all opposition, Cromwell passed laws to strip Irish Catholics of power once and for all. Catholics who owned land east of the River Shannon were forced to hand it over to Cromwell's soldiers and those who had backed him with money. All they got in return were plots of poor land in distant Connaught and Co. Clare.

The new law said that any Irish landowner who did not move by 1st May 1654 would be executed or sent as a slave to the West Indies. The only Catholic Irish allowed to stay were labourers and servants. The saying 'to Hell or to Connaught' entered the language to suggest an impossible choice, and a terrible humiliation.

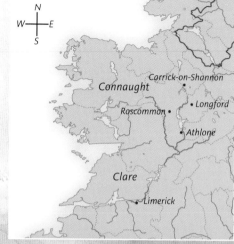

Map showing the route of the River Shannon

About the land

ⓖ Over 11 million acres of land were taken from the Catholic landowners and offered to about 35,000 of Cromwell's soldiers and financial backers.

ⓖ By 1653, almost one third of the population of Ireland in 1640 was dead, in exile or transported into slavery.

ⓖ At the time of the Great Rebellion in 1641 Irish Catholics owned 59% of all the land in the country. By 1685, it was 14%.

44,000 people moved west across the River Shannon in 1653–54.

Another dramatic change

In Ireland as a whole (excluding Connaught and Co. Clare) land ownership – and therefore the ruling class – was now completely Protestant. Many Catholics hoped that, when Charles II was restored to the throne in 1660, he would undo Cromwell's harsh laws. But after 11 years in exile, Charles owed the return of his crown to the same Protestants who had supported Cromwell. He dared not upset them but, in 1685, he died and was followed by James II, a Catholic. He allowed the Irish parliament to meet and overturn Cromwell's land settlement.

But the English would not tolerate a Catholic king and, in 1688, overthrew him in the Glorious Revolution and brought in the Protestant William III. Once again, Irish history was about to change dramatically.

James II

After James II (1633–1701) was thrown out he looked to Scotland for support, but his followers were defeated at the Battle of Dunkeld in 1689. His next stop was Ireland – with a little help from his French friends.

www.bbc.co.uk/history/british/civil_war_revolution/glorious_revolution_01.shtml

Williamite wars

After failing to get support in Scotland, James II arrived at Kinsale with a small French army in 1689. When it came to getting his throne back he was a persistent fellow who wouldn't take no for an answer, even if it meant more fighting and bloodshed. He was hoping that Irish Catholics would help him, and under Richard Talbot, Earl of Tyrconnell, quite a few of them were willing to try...

Within days of James landing, rumours were flying around Ulster that Protestants were being massacred again, as in 1641. The gates of Londonderry were shut against James's army and a long siege of the city began. People were eating dogs, rats, mice and even candles to stay alive by the time it ended 15 weeks later. The cry of 'No Surrender' has been part of Ulster's history ever since.

In 1690, William III arrived with his army and won famous victories at the Battles of the Boyne and of Aughrim. James fled to France and the end for the Irish Catholics came at the Siege of Limerick in 1691. In return for surrendering, the 'Wild Geese' as they were called, were allowed to go into exile and join the French army.

Interesting tactics

☺ The Commanding Officer of Londonderry was about to let James's army in when 13 apprentices slammed the city gates shut. Ulster Protestants still celebrate this every year with the Apprentice Boys' March.

☺ English ships with food and soldiers were waiting offshore throughout the siege, but failed to land them. This made Ulster Protestants believe they must always rely on themselves.

The Battle of the Boyne took place between Oldbridge and Donore Hill, west of Drogheda.

Penal laws

William III promised to return land to those Catholics who stayed, and to give everyone religious freedom, but the promise was not kept. Instead, the Popery (or Penal) Laws of 1704 imposed harsh restrictions.

Catholics could not vote, buy land, set up schools or even own a horse worth over £5. Bishops were banned in the hope that Catholicism would die out, since only bishops could ordain priests. This failed, because so many people supported the faith that the laws could not be enforced. All over the country 'hedge schools' were run in the open air or ruined buildings.

The same laws affected Protestant sects who did not belong to the Irish Anglican Church, such as Ulster Calvinists and Presbyterians. They were called Dissenters, and many left for America.

Unusual facts

Ⓖ An average of 4,000 Ulster Dissenters a year emigrated to America in the 18th century. 10 US Presidents claimed to be descended from them.

Ⓖ In Galway, in 1731, orders were given to expel Catholic friars. They failed, because the friars gave the mayor bottles of wine and he did nothing!

Catholic priests taught (and held services) in 'hedge schools'.

find out more at www.triskelle.eu/history/williamitewar.php

In 1782, Henry Grattan said 'Ireland is now a nation' when the English parliament seemed to give the Irish the right to make Irish laws. But, in practice, it didn't happen.

Lethal landlords

🌀 By law, a Catholic had to leave any land he owned to be divided among all his sons and so, gradually, Catholics owned smaller and smaller strips of land.

🌀 Secret societies of land workers were set up to threaten bad landlords with violence. They gave themselves names like Whiteboys and Defenders. These tactics were used again in the next century.

The Protestant ascendancy

During the 18th century all wealth and power was in the hands of Protestants. Merchants and landowners became rich and, as a result, large parts of Dublin began to be rebuilt. Wide streets and squares replaced the dirty, narrow alleys and by 1800 it was one of the finest cities in Europe – as it still is.

By contrast, most of those in the countryside were crowded into tiny cabins with barely enough to live on. Some died of starvation, especially in 1740–41, years in which the winters were very harsh. All across Europe there was famine as the crops failed. In Ireland almost 400,000 people died. Famines have been a recognised feature of Irish history, caused by poor harvests in times of harsh weather.

Countryside living was in stark contrast to the city life in Dublin.

Ulster is different

In Ulster things were different from the rest of Ireland. Linen weaving was a speciality of the province, and by the end of the century Ulster linen accounted for half of all Irish exports. In 1783 the first cotton mill was set up in Belfast, and Ulster would grow rich from this industrial revolution.

Two important things were happening in Ireland during the last 25 years of the century. There was no longer any fear of a Catholic seizing the English throne and so, very slowly, Irish Catholics began to be given a little more freedom. Meanwhile the Protestants who had settled in Ireland at the beginning of the century wanted more say in running their affairs. They began to demand greater independence – but extraordinary events in France changed everything...

Peep-o'-day boys

Ulster also had secret gangs in the countryside, the best known being the Peep-o'-day boys. In 1795 they set up the first Orange Order Lodge to celebrate the Battle of the Boyne. Within a year there were 90 Lodges.

Cotton mill

People weaving linen

find out more at www.libraryireland.com/Belfast-History/Cotton.php

Failed revolutions 1798–1803

Both Protestant and Catholic Irishmen were thrilled by the success of the Americans in fighting for independence from Britain in 1776. Perhaps the same could happen here? When the French Revolution broke out in 1789 some of them, like the lawyer Wolfe Tone, got very excited.

Theobald Wolfe Tone founded the United Irishmen, a group wanting greater independence from Britain, whatever their religion. In 1798 the United Irishmen began rebellions in several places, whilst Tone persuaded France to send troops to help. The rebels were badly organised, and in any case many Catholics refused to support them. They were defeated, many were killed and most were brutally treated. Wolfe Tone was captured and committed suicide in prison.

Theobald Wolfe Tone
(1763–1798)

In 1803 Robert Emmet, a Dublin Protestant, made a feeble attempt to start another rebellion, and although he was executed his dying speech is remembered: 'When my country takes her place among the nations of the earth...' But by then the Irish parliament had voted 158–115 to support the Act of Union that made Ireland part of the United Kingdom.

Robert Emmet
(1778–1803)

Dreadful battles

🅖 Although Catholics and Protestants sometimes fought side by side there were, once again, horrible massacres – for example at Scullabogue, where 50 Protestants and 20 Catholics were burned or stabbed to death.

🅖 The Battle of Vinegar Hill in June 1798 finally destroyed the rebels. The British army took no prisoners. During the revolts at least 30,000 people – possibly more – were killed.

Act of Union, 1801

Effects of the Union

Independence seemed further away than ever now. Yet many Catholics welcomed the Union because they thought British Protestants would be more tolerant than Irish ones; and most Ulster Protestants welcomed it because they thought Union provided their best guarantee of protection.

Daniel O'Connell
(1775–1847)

One Catholic who opposed it was Daniel O'Connell, 'the Liberator'. He was a natural leader who was opposed to violence but determined to free Catholics from discrimination. For a penny a month people could belong to his Catholic Association, which was organised like a modern political party. Many thousands joined and attended huge, well-behaved meetings. Thanks mainly to these, the Catholic Emancipation Act was passed in 1829 giving Catholics the vote and the right to sit in Parliament. In 1838 taxes paid by Catholics to the Protestant church were abolished.

The Big Wind

In 1831 a cholera epidemic hit Ireland, and on 6th January 1839, 'the Night of the Big Wind' struck. The worst hurricane for centuries destroyed houses, cabins and churches, uprooted trees and killed many.

Nobody counted the exact numbers at O'Connell's meetings, but it was said that in 1843, 300,000 came to hear him at Cashel and at least 750,000 at Tara.

find out more at www.spartacus.schoolnet.co.uk/PRoconnell.htm

O'Connell began pressing for Irish independence, but before he died in 1847 something as bad as the Black Death 500 years earlier began sweeping across the land – An Gorta Mór, the Great Hunger. In his last speech to parliament, O'Connell said: 'I predict that one quarter of the population will perish unless you come to her (Ireland's) relief…'

The Great Famine

In 1845–46 the wind carried potato blight across Europe to Ireland, turning the crops into a stinking, slimy mess. Millions were affected throughout the continent, but it was worst in the south and west of Ireland. 70% of the population had less than five acres and lived only on potatoes and buttermilk. By 1847 few seed potatoes were left to grow future crops, so the effects of the disease spread over five years.

Potato crops were inedible

The government tried to find solutions – soup kitchens and workhouses were set up in 1847 and public work schemes started to provide a small wage for those not already too weak. Some landlords tried to help; others were ruthless, sending wreckers to turn starving families out of their cabins. The suffering and death were appalling.

Ireland's population

Ⓖ The population was 8.2 million in 1841. Official records show that, by 1851, 1.5 million had emigrated, but no-one is sure how many died of starvation. Estimates vary between 880,000 and over a million.

Ⓖ Ireland suffered more than neighbouring regions with the potato blight because of their dependence on the crop and the British government's failure to properly address the crisis.

By August 1847 soup kitchens were feeding 3 million a day, almost half the population. Workhouses were grim places, but even so could only provide for 100,000, less than 20% of what was needed.

Emigration 1845–1921

Even the relief schemes started by the government in 1846–47 were stopped at the end of 1847, long before the potato blight and the suffering were over. In desperation, people began to emigrate, sometimes paying their own fares but often at the expense of landowners happy to get them off their land. 1847 was a black year. Conditions on board some of the boats – the 'coffin ships' – were dreadful and cholera killed many people before they could land in America or Canada.

Of 213,000 people who left Ireland that year, 13,000 died before they arrived. For the rest of the 19th century emigration became a fact of life for people who saw no future at home. Many took with them a hatred of the British government for doing so little to help them.

In the 70 years from 1851 to 1921 another 3 million Irish emigrated abroad – most to America and Canada, but many to Britain, Australia and New Zealand.

The coffin ships

The safety of the ships improved rapidly after 1847 but fire was a constant danger. Between 1847–1853, 53 boats were lost to fire at sea and 9,000 people died.

find out more at www.ego4u.com/en/read-on/countries/ireland/great-famine

Young Ireland and The Nation

The Rising of '48!
Sounds impressive, doesn't it?
Many of Daniel O'Connell's followers had died or emigrated in the famine. Some of the survivors felt desperate, and they wanted action for independence NOW. They felt a Rising was needed. It happened in the cabbage patch of Widow MacCormack's farm in Ballingarry, Co. Tipperary. Two people were killed and a handful lightly wounded – and that was the Rising of '48. It's hardly surprising not much was achieved...

Young Ireland was a movement started by those who felt that although O'Connell had achieved reforms, his peaceful methods could never win political freedom. They published their ideas in a weekly newspaper called The Nation.

James Stephens was a Protestant Young Irelander who escaped abroad from the farce at Ballingarry. He returned in 1856, determined to create a secret society that would not be infiltrated by spies. He also travelled to America looking for men and money, knowing that many who had emigrated in the famine were very bitter about Britain.

James Stephens
(1824–1901)

On the same day in 1858, the Irish Republican Brotherhood (IRB) was launched in Dublin, and the Fenian Brotherhood in New York. Stephens' aim was a major rebellion supported by Irish Americans in 1865.

Fighting facts

☺ Stephens told the Fenian Brotherhood that he had 50,000 guns and 85,000 Irishmen ready to rebel in 1865. In addition, he said, 15,000 members of the British Army would join in. This was just wishful thinking.

☺ In November 1865, Stephens was betrayed and arrested. He escaped from prison but the IRB sacked him as their leader and he fled to France.

The Nation newspaper

Fenian violence

The Fenians, as members of the IRB were now called, laid new plans for rebellion in 1867. Once again the plans were betrayed, and although there were small pockets of fighting, it proved to be another fiasco. But two events in England created four Fenian 'martyrs'.

In Manchester, three Irishmen were accused of killing a policeman during the rescue of two arrested Fenians, and hanged; and in London an explosion at Clerkenwell prison during the attempted escape of another Fenian killed 30 people and badly injured many more. An Irishman named Michael Barrett was hanged for this. To people in Britain these events brought home the importance of the Irish question; in Ireland the four martyrs became part of the Fenian mythology that lasted through the 20th century.

Irish Republican Army

In 1866 a group of Irish emigrants under John O'Neill invaded Canada, then part of the British Empire. They called themselves the Irish Republican Army, but were quickly driven out.

Michael O'Brien Michael Larkin William Allen

Clerkenwell prison

The execution of Allen, Larkin and O'Brien for the 1867 Manchester killing caused particular bitterness in Ireland and America because none of them had fired the fatal shot.

Michael Barrett was the last man to be publicly hanged in Great Britain.

find out more at http://freepages.genealogy.rootsweb.ancestry.com/~mruddy/fenian3.htm

The Land League and the Land War

For many years there had been unrest because of the high rents that small tenant farmers paid for poor land. In 1879 Michael Davitt founded the National Land League with Charles Stewart Parnell as its President. After a harsh winter it seemed as if famine was returning, and that tenants might again be forced off their land by unsympathetic landlords. For several years the Land War raged, as barns were burned down and landlords and farm managers were attacked.

Michael Davitt
(1846–1906)

Interesting facts

⑤ In **1880** Captain Boycott refused to lower his tenants' rent, and evicted them. In return, workers refused to gather the harvest and local people ignored him. 'Boycott' became a new word in the language.

⑤ In **1881**, Parnell was sent to Kilmainham Jail, accused of encouraging violence during the Land War period. His agreement with Gladstone was reached from prison, and became known as the Kilmainham Treaty.

The Land War lasted from 1879 to the 1881 Kilmainham Treaty.

The need for reform united republicans, backers of Home Rule, American Fenians (who sent money) and even the anti-Fenian Church. This gave Parnell the power to persuade the Prime Minister, William Gladstone, to pass the Land Act in 1881, guaranteeing fair rent, fixed tenancy and the right to sell.

Focus on Ulster

In the second half of the 19th century Ulster grew into Ireland's main industrial centre – and Protestants owned the majority of its industries. It became famous for its textiles (linen and clothing), its engineering and its shipbuilding yards.

The rest of Ireland was still mainly agricultural, so Ulster depended on Britain as the main market through which its goods were sent on to the rest of the world. But at the same time there was often fighting on the streets between Catholics and Protestants, and sectarian divisions were growing worse. Most Protestants were determined to remain united with Britain (Unionists) and rejected the idea of an independent Ireland. They feared the domination of Catholics south of the border who, they believed, had no understanding of their industrial economy.

In the early days Belfast was a small town of a few thousand people. By 1841 it had grown to 70,000, and by 1901 the population was nearly 350,000.

The Titanic

The ill-fated Titanic was one of the largest ships built in Ulster's shipyards. Its last port of call on its maiden voyage in 1912 was Queenstown (Cobh). Three days later it hit an iceberg and 1,517 people died.

find out more at www.thelandleague.org/history.asp

The Home Rule issue

The Home Rule Association was formed in 1870, and won the majority of Irish seats in elections to the British parliament. For the first few years its members spent more time arguing with each other than anything else! But once Parnell took over as leader in 1879, the same year he became president of the Land League, things began to make progress.

Home Rule was the idea that Ireland would make its own laws in its own parliament, but would remain part of the United Kingdom.

In London Gladstone knew that the Land Act was only a first step in finding solutions to the 'Irish Question'. Parnell turned the Irish MPs into a disciplined group called the Irish Parliamentary Party to keep the pressure on Gladstone and his Liberal Party. But too many of the Liberals were opposed to Home Rule and, when Gladstone proposed it in 1886, his party split and was defeated in elections.

When Gladstone returned to power he tried again in 1893, and again he was defeated. The Conservatives replaced the Liberals and sided with the Ulster Unionists against Home Rule. But by then Parnell was dead.

Gladstone speaking at a Home Rule debate

Charles Stewart Parnell

Kitty O'Shea

Ⓢ Parnell had been living with Kitty, the wife of an Irish MP called Captain O'Shea. In 1889 O'Shea demanded a divorce. Parnell's reputation was ruined, and many in his party abandoned him.

Ⓢ Parnell died in 1891 and was given a magnificent funeral in Dublin. Thirty different bands played as his coffin passed along the streets in pouring rain, and at least 200,000 Catholics and Protestants were there.

Promoting Irishness

Even as the idea of Home Rule was being pursued, there were many who wanted to build a feeling of self-confidence and pride in being Irish. Scholars looked back to the Gaelic past – to the language and the old Brehon laws, and to the legends and history written down by the monks. In 1884 the Gaelic Athletic Association (GAA) was set up to promote nationalism and encourage ancient sports like athletics, hurling and handball.

In 1893 the Gaelic League was founded to promote Irish as the national language and to encourage Irish cultural activities such as dancing, music, poetry. By 1904 the League had 593 branches and 50,000 members.

The legend of Setanta and the hound of Cuchulain promoted the distant origins of hurling.

Irish dancing is popular. *Riverdance* and *Lord of the Dance* have helped to modernise it and spread it worldwide.

Dublin's historic Croke Park was renovated in the 1990s. In February 2007 Ireland played their first rugby match there, against France in the Six Nations tournament.

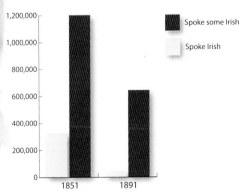

In 1851, 319,600 people spoke only Irish and over 1.2 million spoke some. 40 years later, only 38,200 had Irish as their only language, and 642,000 spoke a little.

find out more at www.gaa.ie/page/about_the_gaa.html

'Ulster will fight and Ulster will be right!'

Gladstone's attempts to give Ireland Home Rule led to threats of civil war in Ulster. When the 1886 Home Rule bill was suggested, advertisements appeared in newspapers asking for rifles, and men began military training. In Britain the Conservative party played what they called the 'Orange card' in order to defeat Gladstone's Liberals – in other words, they took the side of the Orange Order in Ulster and encouraged a belief that rebellion could be successful.

Newspaper advertisement looking for rifles

Home Rule bill

🅖 Another Home Rule bill was suggested in 1911. The following year a large military body, the Ulster Volunteer Force, was formed, and over 200,000 people signed the Ulster Solemn League and Covenant to use any means to defeat Home Rule.

🅖 Despite this, the Home Rule bill was passed in 1912 and became law on 18th September 1914 – but by then World War I had begun.

When the 1886 bill was defeated, Unionist street celebrations were so wild that several people were killed in Belfast. The same strong opposition happened between 1892–93. The Home Rule issue then went quiet for 17 years, but the idea that Ulster would fight to the death against it was set hard in people's minds.

Ulster Unionist street celebrations turned violent.

War clouds gather

In the early years of the 20th century the conditions of industrial workers in Dublin were terrible. Jim Larkin, leader of the Irish Transport and General Workers' Union, organised a strike in 1913 which ended in a 5-month lock-out lasting into 1914.

When Larkin was arrested the socialist James Connolly, who saw independence and workers' rights as the same thing, took over leadership. He founded the Irish Citizen Army, training the workers to fight but keeping in mind their usefulness in fighting for Irish independence later.

Yet when World War I began in August 1914, 100,000 Irishmen flocked to join the British Army in the first year alone. Half came from Ulster and half from south of the present border, and all fought with great bravery.

Poster advertisement to encourage Irish men to join the British Army

Jim Larkin
(1876–1947)

45 Irish soldiers won Britain's highest award for bravery, the Victoria Cross, during WWI. 38 of the Royal Flying Corps' top aces were Irish.

Living standards

In 1913 a third of Dublin's population lived in one-room apartments without light, water or toilets, and average pay was 12% below the poverty line. The death rate was the highest of any city in Europe.

find out more at www.spartacus.schoolnet.co.uk/IRElarkin.htm

The Easter Rising of 1916

There were others in the Irish Volunteers and Connolly's Citizen Army who thought that 'England's difficulty was Ireland's opportunity'. They planned to remain strong and demand Home Rule after the war.

A small group was not willing to wait. It smuggled weapons into the country and its leader, Patrick Pearse, set a date for a rising in Dublin – Easter Sunday, 1916. Although he hoped 10,000 would rebel, there were only about a thousand on the day. They shut themselves into the Post Office and other buildings, but a gunboat in the Liffey shelled them into surrender. The rising was unpopular with ordinary Dubliners. The captured rebels were jeered as they were marched away, but the British foolishly executed 15 of the leaders, and this turned the Irish mood the other way.

Patrick Pearse
(1879–1916)

When World War I began, the leaders of the different groups agreed to postpone Home Rule until it was over. Both nationalists from the Irish Volunteers and unionists from the Ulster Volunteer Force fought in the British Army. Over 35,000 were killed during the war. They all expected to be rewarded for their loyalty when peace returned, but by then events had moved on swiftly.

Difficult times

☺ Many returning servicemen were victimised when they came home to Ireland in 1919. 200 were murdered and many found it difficult to get jobs – unemployment among ex-servicemen was 46% in Ireland, but 10% in Britain.

The General Post Office building still stands in O'Connell Street today.

War of Independence 1919–1921

Eamon de Valera headed the political party Sinn Féin (meaning 'Ourselves Alone'), first set up in 1905, while Michael Collins began to organise the IRA for the war he knew would come. In the British general election of December 1918, Sinn Féin won 70% of the Irish seats, and immediately declared itself to be the Dáil Éireann, the Irish parliament.

The same day two Irish policemen were murdered, and the Troubles began. At first, fellow Irish policemen were the main targets of the IRA, but things turned even nastier when the British sent in soldiers called Black and Tans. Their first revenge attacks took place in Limerick and they got their nickname from a pack of hunting hounds there. Now both sides were involved in violent conflict.

New leaders

ⓖ Eamon de Valera was one of the leaders sentenced to be executed, but because he was an American citizen he was imprisoned instead. He was released in 1917.

Eamon de Valera (1882–1975)

ⓖ By the end of 1917, new leaders like de Valera and Michael Collins were making plans for independence. The Irish Volunteers and the Citizen Army merged into the IRA, the Irish Republican Army.

Michael Collins (1890–1922)

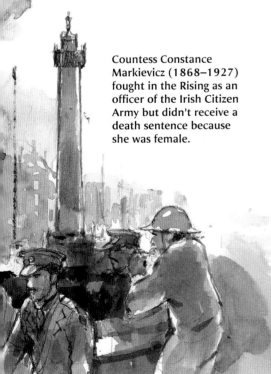
Countess Constance Markievicz (1868–1927) fought in the Rising as an officer of the Irish Citizen Army but didn't receive a death sentence because she was female.

On 21st November 1920 Michael Collins ordered the IRA to murder 11 men he believed to be spies. They and three British soldiers were shot.

The same afternoon, the Black and Tans took their revenge by driving armoured cars into Croke Park and killing 11 spectators and a player at a Gaelic football match.

d out more at www.irishtourist.com/general_information/history_of_ireland/1916_easter_rising.shtml

Anglo-Irish Treaty 1921

Throughout 1920 the war got bloodier. Both sides carried out killings and revenge attacks. The mayor of Cork was murdered in his own home and the centre of the city was burned down. The British Prime Minister, David Lloyd George, opened negotiations in 1921 but, by then, the Protestant majority in six of the Ulster counties had made it clear they would remain within Britain. Opinion in the south was divided between those who refused to accept anything less than complete independence, and those willing to accept limited independence to begin with and win complete freedom later.

After failed negotiations with de Valera in July 1921, Lloyd George met an Irish team led by Michael Collins and Arthur Griffith and, in December, the Anglo-Irish Treaty was signed.

The Anglo-Irish Treaty was signed on 6th December 1921. A 'Free State' was offered as part of the agreement.

Times of negotiation

Ⓖ On 24th December 1920 the British parliament passed an Act for the partition of Ireland. Six counties of Ulster now had Home Rule – the very thing they had once opposed – under their first Prime Minister, Sir James Craig.

James Craig
(1871–1940)

Ⓖ Before negotiating with de Valera the British government offered a truce on 11th July 1921. It came just in time for Michael Collins who believed the IRA was exhausted and could only last another three weeks. After 18 months 1,500 people from both sides had died.

Civil War 1922–23

After signing the Treaty, Collins said he had got something Ireland had wanted for seven hundred years. But, he asked, 'Will anyone be satisfied? I tell you this: I signed my death warrant.' The Treaty gave 26 of the 32 counties complete control of their own affairs at home and abroad – but with King George V as the named head of state.

The Dáil voted 64–57 to accept the Treaty, but de Valera opposed it and resigned to form a new party, Fianna Fáil. The IRA split down the middle and almost at once civil war broke out between the two sides. The fighting was as brutal as during the War of Independence, and although the pro-Treaty side won, the feeling of betrayal and bitterness lasted for decades.

King George V
(1865–1936)

Shocking fact

ⓖ 77 anti-Treaty republicans were executed in prison between November 1922 and May 1923, including Erskine Childers (whose son would become President in 1973–74).

Michael Collins' prediction came true. In August 1922 he was ambushed and shot at Béal na mBláth. Most of Ireland was shocked but the bitterness had become so great that some rejoiced.

find out more at www.moreorless.au.com/heroes/collins.html

Reconstruction in the south

It was a huge job to rebuild Ireland after all the fighting between 1916 and 1923. Railways, bridges and buildings had to be repaired. A brand new central government had to be organised to run everything from Dublin instead of London. New schools and education systems had to be established, a proper police force set up and a new legal system introduced. An industrial base had to be built in independent Ireland because most industry was in Ulster.

This was not easy during the economic depression that hit the world in 1929 and lasted for years. But in 1932, de Valera's Fianna Fáil won the elections. In 1936 the IRA was made illegal, and in 1937 a new constitution gave the state a new name – Éire.

> That half of the IRA that had been fighting for the unity of Ireland and complete separation from Britain lost both of those things in the civil war. Some members despaired and emigrated to America, some continued to set off bombs and some, like Eamon de Valera, played a patient political game...

Map showing the four provinces and 32 counties of Ireland

	Ulster
	Connaught
	Leinster
	Munster

Political literature of the time

Ⓖ Dublin born poet William Butler Yeats (1865–1939) was moved by the events of the Easter Rising. He wrote *Easter 1916* soon after.

Ⓖ In 1922 James Joyce's (1882–1941) tale *Ulysses* was banned from publication.

Ⓖ When Sean O'Casey's (1880–1964) play *The Plough and the Stars* (1926) was first performed there were riots because it showed unheroic IRA men.

Fianna Fáil won the elections in 1932.

Éire put a great deal of time and energy into rebuilding its infrastructure.

'What we have we hold'

In 1921, the population of Ulster was two thirds Protestant. When the Free State was founded, they saw their enemies as those in the IRA still fighting for a united Ireland. So, keeping the borders of Ulster was important to them.

In the early years, however, the Ulster Catholics thought Ireland would soon be reunited, and did not co-operate with the Unionists. This led many Protestants to believe that the Catholics wanted Ulster to fail. Even though Ulster's economy was not hit too badly by the world depression, Catholics were still denied fair housing, jobs and voting rights.

This state of affairs would last for 50 years and more, so it was not surprising that Ulster Catholics came to believe the division of Ireland must be ended.

Life at the time

☞ In 1922, 232 people were killed and nearly a thousand injured in shootings and riots in Belfast. Nearly 400 IRA members were imprisoned and the Royal Ulster Constabulary (which was seen as anti-Catholic) was set up.

☞ By 1926 the population, which had been 6.5 million in 1851, had fallen to 4.2 million (2.9 million of them in Éire). 43% of men and women born in Ireland were living abroad.

☞ In 1937, 83% of the houses in the Ulster countryside still had no running water.

find out more at www.apostles.com/devalera.html

The Emergency and after

The new constitution (laws of government) cut Éire's last links with the British crown. The country was a republic in all but name – but to use the word officially made political unity with Northern Ireland more difficult than ever.

John Costello
(1891–1976)

When World War II started in 1939 it was called 'The Emergency' and Éire remained neutral (not helping or supporting either side). To most people this proved they were truly independent at last, although it did not stop many thousands of Irish joining the British Army to fight Hitler.

In 1948, Fianna Fáil lost power and the new coalition government, a union formed between different parties, did what de Valera had not dared – it declared all Ireland a republic, with John Costello as its Taoiseach. The North might not yet be willing to join this republic – but perhaps one day...?

Breathtaking facts

☉ During World War II over 50,000 Irish people served in the British armed services. Another 93,000 emigrated, mainly to Britain to work in the docks and arms factories.

☉ The IRA had few members by 1939, but it carried out a bombing campaign in England. De Valera was furious because this broke the policy of neutrality, and during the Emergency years nine IRA men were executed.

Although the Irish Republic remained neutral during World War II, many of the Irish involved were part of the navy and kept guard over British waters.

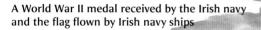

A World War II medal received by the Irish navy and the flag flown by Irish navy ships

No end to emigration

In the 1950s there were many fine achievements. Record numbers of new houses were built, electricity now reached most people and medical services were greatly improved. Yet still people left the country.

The government wanted to build up industry to provide everything Ireland needed, so it discouraged foreign companies from coming. This policy didn't really work and there were not nearly enough opportunities, particularly for the young. Everything seemed a bit old-fashioned and nothing much seemed to change in daily life. The population, which by 1926 had already dropped to 2.9 million in Éire, just carried on falling. From 1951 to 1956, on average, 39,350 people left every year. The years between 1956 and 1961 were even worse, and 42,400 left annually. Something had to be done...

Medical services were starting to get better for Irish citizens.

About population

Ⓖ In 1953 the Health Act provided free medical services for those unable to pay for them. In 1958, 28.5% of the population of Éire qualified for them.

Ⓖ By 1961 the population of Éire was 2.8 million, the lowest it had ever been.

find out more at www.secondworldwarni.org/default.aspx?id=3&timelineid=1

Turning the corner

**Seán Lemass
(1899–1971)**

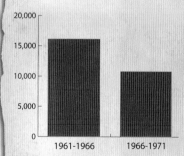

If you'd stood in a Dublin street at the end of the Emergency and told them what life would be like in 60 years time they could not have believed the changes Ireland was about to enjoy...

In 1959 Seán Lemass took over from de Valera as Taoiseach and things quickly began to change. The old idea that companies in the Republic could make everything the country wanted had failed. So foreigners were offered advantages to come and set up companies. Ireland, like Britain, needed to earn foreign money by selling overseas, so companies that sold their goods abroad were given further advantages.

This new approach soon began to work, and by 1966 exports from the 26 counties were nearly 60% higher than in 1929. This meant there were more jobs and wages were going up. For the first time in living memory, there was a sense of hope. Year by year emigration fell and the population began to grow again.

In the Republic

Ⓖ From 1961 to 1966, the numbers of people leaving the Republic fell to an average 16,120 a year; from 1966 to 1971 it was down to 10,780 a year.

Ⓖ By 1971, the birth rate had been increasing for ten years. The population was nearly 3 million – back above the level of 1929.

A snapshot of O'Connell Street, Dublin in 1944

The spire of Dublin, officially called the Monument of Light, is 120m tall and was finished in 2003.

A snapshot of O'Connell Street, Dublin in the new millennium

Church power declines

In 1937 the new constitution had given the Roman Catholic Church a special position in Éire. To the Church, this meant that only it could decide how people should behave.

In 1950, the government wanted to give free health care to all mothers and children under 16, but the Church opposed it. They said it would destroy proper family life and encourage bad behaviour. This caused a good deal of public anger, but the government would not go against the Church.

One of the results was that by the middle of the 1970s the influence of the Church had declined greatly. People could afford to live better now. They looked outwards to the rest of Europe and were no longer prepared to put up with outdated views.

In the 1950s there were three priests for every parish in Éire but now there are not enough to look after them all. In 2007, 160 priests died and only nine new ones were ordained.

find out more at www.inyourpocket.com/ireland/dublin//feature/70271-Dublin__A_Short_History.html

Joining the rest of Europe

In the 1960s half of Ireland's imports came from Britain, and nearly half of her exports went there. So it made sense for both countries to apply together for membership of the Common Market, as it was called then. They had to wait until 1973 but, particularly for Ireland, it was worth it.

Currency changes from Punt to Euro

By the 1990s it was being called the 'Celtic Tiger' as new businesses and industries were set up in Ireland and brought prosperity by selling to the rest of Europe and the world. Yet Irish agriculture still provided 85% of the food Ireland needed. People began to earn wages and salaries their grandparents could only have dreamed of. Living standards in Ireland went from being one of the worst in Europe to the second best.

The Celtic Tiger

By 1990, 50% of the Republic's foreign sales and 25% of her imports were to and from members of the European Union other than Britain.

US hi-tech companies in Ireland like the fact that transatlantic time differences mean work can be done here in the morning with the results being on American desks for the start of their working day.

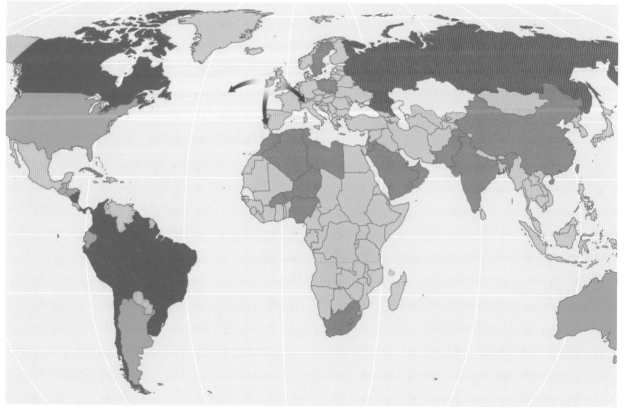

This shows Ireland's position on a world map. By the 1990s there was a big increase in imports to and exports from Ireland

Modern Ireland

Ireland today is very different from the rural, conservative country that the revolutionaries fought for between 1916 and 1923. Now it is creative, energetic and self-confident, a country of farmers, bankers and businessmen; of actors, musicians, writers, sportsmen and sportswomen...

United Nations flag

Internationally it plays its part while being careful to remain neutral – for example its soldiers have taken part in many United Nations peace-keeping operations, and from 1997–2002 Mary Robinson, the former President, was the UN's High Commissioner for Human Rights. Modern Ireland is multicultural with over three-quarters of a million immigrants, especially from eastern Europe and Asia, making their living there.

Mary Robinson (1944–present)

Emigration has risen again, but whereas in the past desperate people left to seek a new life, nowadays they go to pursue successful international careers.

Singers Bono and Bob Geldof promote Fair Trade with the UN.

find out more at www.en.wikipedia.org/wiki/Celtic_Tiger

One more twist on our journey through Irish history in order to bring us up to date. This time we're back in Northern Ireland...

The Troubles begin

As you read earlier, Catholics in Northern Ireland had been treated unfairly for years and in the 1960s they began to do something about it. They started to copy the civil rights protests that black Americans were waging in the USA and in 1967 the Civil Rights Association was formed. Meetings and marches soon turned into riots and the first bombs went off in 1969. British troops were sent there and, at first, the Catholic minority saw the soldiers as protectors.

Then, on 30th January 1972, came Bloody Sunday in Derry when the troops thought they were being shot at. In the violence, thirteen people died. It was a turning point. Now the Catholic minority believed that only the IRA could protect them.

More Trouble

Ⓖ 1972 was the worst year of The Troubles. A total of 467 people died violently.

Ⓖ Between 1971–75 over 2,000 people, mainly Catholics, were imprisoned without trial. This helped the IRA recruit people to attack Protestants.

There were lots of arrests at the Civil Rights Association march.

Violence grows

The Northern Ireland government broke down because of the violence, and the British government introduced direct rule from London. This was only meant to last a short time until a better system was worked out, but when proposals for a new government were announced in 1974 the Unionists (mainly Protestants) were furious.

A 15-day general strike brought the country to a standstill, making it even more difficult for industries and businesses to operate in Ulster. In the end, direct rule went on for 30 years.

In the meantime the IRA carried on a violent policy of bombings and shootings, and in answer the Protestants formed their own terrorist force, the UVF (Ulster Volunteer Force). During the troubles over 3,300 people were murdered, and 38,000 injured.

UVF mural on the side of a brick house

IRA mural on the side of a brick house

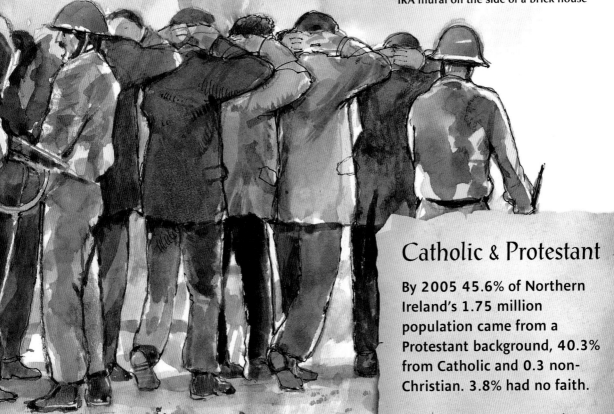

Catholic & Protestant

By 2005 45.6% of Northern Ireland's 1.75 million population came from a Protestant background, 40.3% from Catholic and 0.3 non-Christian. 3.8% had no faith.

find out more at www.triskelle.eu/history/civilrightsmovement.php?index=060.170.030

Slow steps to peace

In 1985 Britain and Éire signed the Anglo-Irish agreement. For the first time, the Republic recognised the right of Northern Ireland to be part of the United Kingdom. Britain agreed that Ireland should be united if a majority of the people of Ulster voted for it.

New ways had to be found to end the IRA's non-stop violence, and to persuade hard-line Protestants to stop preventing change of any kind. It took ten more years but, pushed by the American government, Sinn Féin (the political wing of the IRA) began secret talks with Britain. It finally decided that violence would never result in a united Ireland.

At last, in 1998, the Nationalists and Unionists agreed to run Northern Ireland together, and signed the Good Friday Agreement.

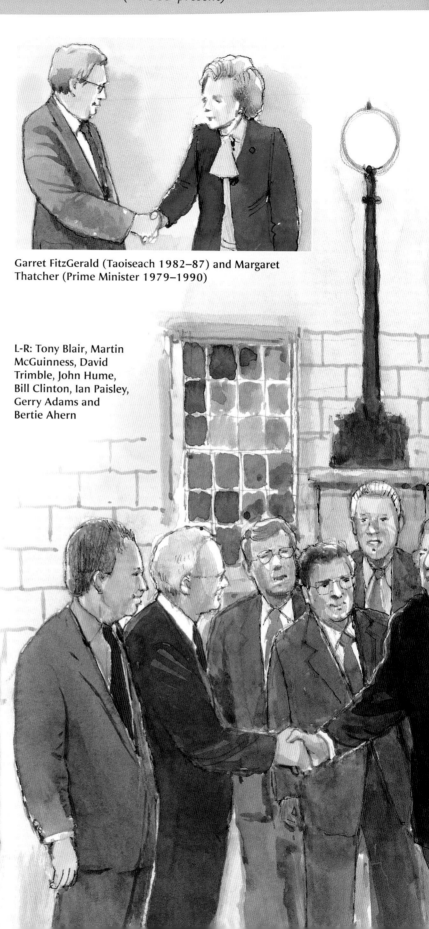

Garret FitzGerald (Taoiseach 1982–87) and Margaret Thatcher (Prime Minister 1979–1990)

L-R: Tony Blair, Martin McGuinness, David Trimble, John Hume, Bill Clinton, Ian Paisley, Gerry Adams and Bertie Ahern

Good Friday Agreement

People north and south of the border voted on the Good Friday Agreement in a referendum. In Northern Ireland 71% voted in favour, and in the Republic 94%.

A bright future

Despite the high hopes of 1998, it took more years before the terrorists on both sides felt safe enough to destroy their weapons. It also took time for the leading Nationalists (Sinn Féin) and Unionists (the Democratic Unionist Party) to trust each other and agree what jobs each would have in the new government. But people could see the bright light at the end of the long dark tunnel of killing.

New businesses began setting up in Ulster, and most of the barriers that had divided communities came down. 8th May 2007 was a red-letter day. The new-look Northern Ireland Assembly met for the first time under its First Minister, Ian Paisley, and its Deputy First Minister, Martin McGuinness. In the 21st century, the island of Ireland could look forward to peace and prosperity.

So there you are. In the space of just a few pages I've shown you some of the ups and downs, the comings and goings and the heroes and villains of Irish history. It's quite a story, isn't it?

Peace people

ⓖ US President Bill Clinton visited Belfast twice, in 1994 and again in 1998.

ⓖ In 1998 the Nobel Peace Prize was awarded to John Hume and David Trimble, leaders of the two main political parties in Northern Ireland.

Peace statue, Derry

Stormont opened in 1932 in Belfast. It is the building where the new Northern Ireland Assembly holds its meetings.

IRA weapons were offered up. It took a long time, but it was seen as a big step towards peace.

find out more at http://news.bbc.co.uk/hi/english/static/northern_ireland/understanding/default.stm

Index

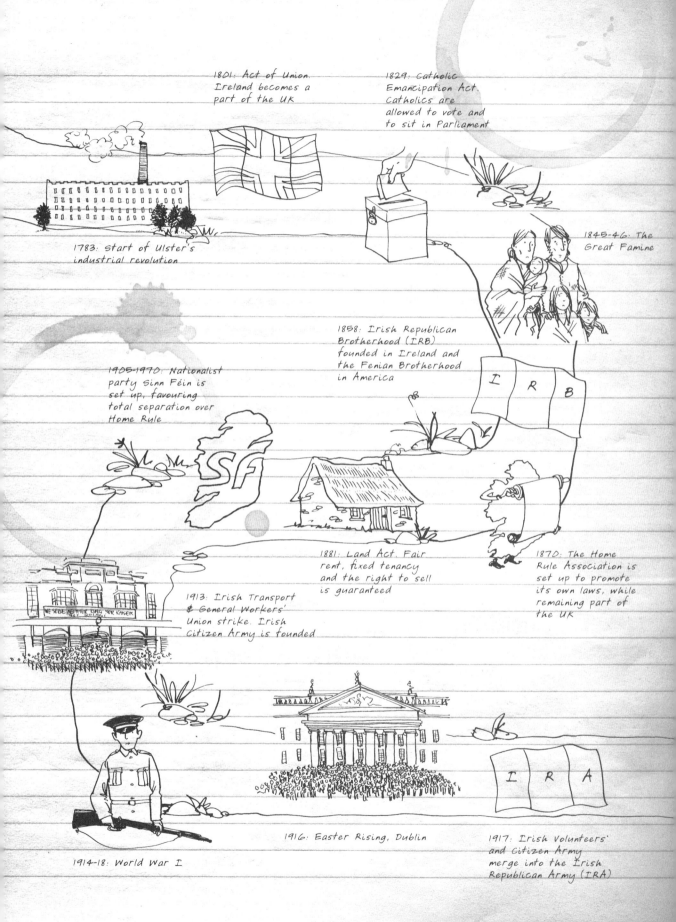

1801: Act of Union. Ireland becomes a part of the UK

1829: Catholic Emancipation Act. Catholics are allowed to vote and to sit in Parliament

1783: start of Ulster's industrial revolution

1845-46: The Great Famine

1858: Irish Republican Brotherhood (IRB) founded in Ireland and the Fenian Brotherhood in America

1905-1970: Nationalist party Sinn Féin is set up, favouring total separation over Home Rule

1881: Land Act. Fair rent, fixed tenancy and the right to sell is guaranteed

1870: The Home Rule Association is set up to promote its own laws, while remaining part of the UK

1913: Irish Transport & General Workers' Union strike. Irish Citizen Army is founded

1914-18: World War I

1916: Easter Rising, Dublin

1917: Irish Volunteers' and Citizen Army merge into the Irish Republican Army (IRA)